I0481565

CRYPTOCURRENCY MINING

The Ultimate Guide to Understanding Bitcoin, Ethereum, and Litecoin Mining

By Sam Sutton

~~~

TABLE OF CONTENTS

Congratulations on downloading your personal copy of *Cryptocurrency Mining*. Thank you for doing so.

Welcome to the ultimate cryptocurrency mining guide. If you are a newcomer to the cryptocurrency world, and you're interested in mining, this is perfect for you. You might only be curious about the workings of cryptocurrencies, and this is a perfect primer.

There are a lot of online resources for cryptocurrencies, and many of them tend to be difficult to understand. They are filled to the brim with abbreviations, technical details, and jargon that a beginner may find it hard to decipher. The following chapters were written with beginners in mind. We've done our best to keep the technical jargon to a minimum.

In order to begin mining, reading this book is a good first step, but your research shouldn't stop here. As you start to build you mining rig, or computer, you need to do more research. There are a lot of individual parts that go into mining, so let's dive in.

There are plenty of books on this subject on the market, thanks again for choosing this one! Every effort was made to ensure it is full of as much useful information as possible. Please enjoy!

BITCOIN, ETHEREUM AND BEYOND: WHAT IS CRYPTOCURRENCY

Cryptocurrency is a virtual or digital currency that provides security for its users by using cryptography. This security feature makes it hard to counterfeit. It most endearing feature is it is organic by nature meaning it does not get issued by a central authority. This makes it immune to any manipulation or interference by the government.

Due to cryptocurrency's anonymous nature, it makes them targets for criminal activities like tax evasion and money laundering.

Bitcoin was the first cryptocurrency to catch the public's attention. Bitcoin was created in 2009 by either an individual or group that called themselves Satoshi Nakamoto. By September 2015, over 14.6 million Bitcoins were already in circulation. These Bitcoins have a market value of about $3.4 billion. The success of Bitcoin has resulted in more cryptocurrencies being created like PPCoin, Namecoin, and Litecoin.

Drawbacks and Benefits

It is easy to transfer money between two people with cryptocurrency. Transfers are expedited by using private and public keys to help with security. The transfers are completed with very low fees, and this lets users stay away from the large fees that many financial institutions and banks will charge to do wire transfers.

At the center of Bitcoin is its blockchain that it stores all the transactions on. Every Bitcoin transaction that has ever been done will be on this blockchain. This gives a data structure that could be exposed to threats from hackers. It can be copied on any computer that runs Bitcoin software. Most experts view blockchain as being important to technologies like crowdfunding and online voting. Cryptocurrencies can even help lower processing fees.

Since cryptocurrencies don't have a central repository and are virtual, the currency can disappear if your computer crashes and you don't have a copy of your total currency. The amount a cryptocurrency can be exchanged for a different currency fluctuates a lot because prices change due to demand and supply.

These cryptocurrencies are not immune to hacking. In the short time, Bitcoin has been around, it has had 40 thefts. A few of these thefts were valued at over one million dollars. Many die-hard fans think cryptocurrencies is a currency that will hold its value, expedites exchange, is easier to move than hard metals, and government and central banks can't touch it.

Satoshi

Satoshi is the smallest unit of Bitcoin currency. It gets its name from the creator of Bitcoin, Satoshi Nakamoto. Cryptocurrencies only exist in the virtual world, unlike physical currencies like the US dollar or the British pound. A cryptocurrency can be broken up into smaller units like the dollar is broken down into cents and a pound is broken down into pence.

Bitcoin

Bitcoin follows ideas that were written in a white paper by Satoshi Nakamoto. This person or group's identity has never been verified. With the offer of lower transaction fees and being operated by a decentralized authority, it is no wonder why Bitcoin has risen to fame. The market cap for every bitcoin that is in circulation is over $7 billion.

You cannot physically hold bitcoins. The balance is stored in a public ledger along with every Bitcoin transaction in the cloud. Each transaction gets verified by huge amounts of computing power. Governments or banks can't back or issue Bitcoins, and they aren't valued as a commodity. In spite of being a legal tender, Bitcoins has triggered the creation of other currencies known as Altcoins.

Bitcoin's balances are stored in private and public keys that are long strings of letters and numbers that are linked by a mathematical algorithm that encrypts them. The public key is equivalent to a bank account number. This is the address that is published to everyone and where other people can send Bitcoins. Private keys are equivalent to a PIN number and need to be kept a secret. It is only used to authorize Bitcoin transfers.

Satoshi Nakamoto

This entity is the pioneer of cryptocurrency. Satoshi Nakamoto is the biggest enigma in cryptocurrency. It is still not clear if it is a she, he, a person, or a group. What we do know is Satoshi Nakamoto published a paper in 2008 that started the creation of cryptocurrency.

Bitcoin Cash

This is a fork of the Bitcoin Classic that became known in August 2017. This cryptocurrency can increase the block size and allows more transactions to be processed.

Since it was launched, Bitcoin has faced pressure from members of its community about scalability. Its block size which is one megabyte or one million bytes was set in 210. It slows down processing time and limits Bitcoin's potential just when it was getting popular. The limit of block size was put into the code to prevent attacks on the network when its value was very low. The value of Bitcoin has gone up substantially, and its block size has gone up to 600 bytes. This creates a scenario where transaction times would cause delays due to more blocks reaching maximum capacity.

Digital Copy

This is a record of every Bitcoin transaction that has been confirmed and was sent to the peer to peer network. This is a security feature on the Bitcoin platform that was created to help with double spending.

With the rise of cryptocurrencies, it also created a problem called double spending. This happens when a user buys something from two sellers and uses the same Bitcoins. This would be like trying to buy apples from two different vendors but using the same money for each transaction. This just can't happen. To solve this problem, Bitcoin's creators made a process where every transaction gets copied into a ledger and is verified by many different Bitcoin miners that are distributed throughout the network.

Each transaction gets recorded into the blockchain then copied and stored digitally across various networks within the decentralized system. To keep users from spending the same money twice, digital copy makes sure each participant has an encrypted digital copy of everybody's holding. Miners will verify each transaction and add them to the ledgers. By having digital copies in the Bitcoin ledgers, it is impossible for the history of transactions to get compromised. Any user that tries to change a transaction within the ledger for their own gain will not be successful since they can only change their own digital copy. In order for a transaction to be changed in the ledger, the user needs to have access to everybody's copy. This would prove to be very futile.

Bitcoin Unlimited

This is an upgrade to Bitcoin Core that gives larger block sizes. It was created to improve transaction speeds. Several improvements to this software have been proposed. These upgrades focus on increasing how many transactions that the system can do by increasing the size of blocks or speeding up the process.

Blocks are files where the Bitcoin transactions are stored. Every time a block gets completed, it gets put into the blockchain. Blocks are limited in size to one megabyte. Bitcoin Unlimited wants to increase the block size. This means that companies and individuals give the computing power that is needed to keep the records of all the transactions.

Since Bitcoins isn't controlled by a central authority, decisions about upgrades are made through a consensus. Any person or organization that pushes a change forward and the other members didn't agree to it can cause a fork in Bitcoin. This means the network that is running Bitcoin will split. Having a consensus-driven approach could make it hard to tackle issues that Bitcoin faces.

Problems with forking are one reason why Bitcoin Unlimited isn't the new standard. Having larger blocks can result in miners who have larger processing units will be more powerful and profitable, while small miners could get pushed out entirely.

Litecoin

Litecoin was created in 2011. It is a different cryptocurrency that is modeled after Bitcoin. Litecoin's creator is Charlie Lee. He is a graduate of MIT and used to work at Google. Litecoin just like Bitcoin is an open source network that is decentralized. It is different than Bitcoin because it can create blocks faster and uses scrypt as proof of work.

Litecoin was created with the hope of being the left to Bitcoin's right. It has gained popularity since it was created. Litecoin is also a peer to peer network. Litecoin was created to improve on Bitcoin's shortcomings. It has earned support as well as liquidity and trade volume. Litecoin was designed to create more coins faster. Litecoin is considered second to Bitcoin, but Litecoins are easier to get and send.

Altcoin

These are all the different cryptocurrencies that have been created after Bitcoin. They say they are better than Bitcoin, but that is still to be seen. Many alternative coins are targeting the limits that Bitcoin has and creating newer versions. There are many varieties of Altcoins.

Most of the Altcoins are built on Bitcoin's framework and makes the peer-to-peer as well. Some offer more efficient and cheaper ways to send transactions. Even though many features of the Altcoins overlap, they are still very different from each other.

Even with all these competitors, Bitcoin is still the leader in the cryptocurrency pack. Newer versions are being launched. This offer changes in areas such as DNS resolution, proof of stake, privacy, transactions speed, and so much more. Some have gained popularity. Some are not as well knows. Some examples of Altcoins are Novacoin, Zetacoin, Feathercoin, Peercoin, Dogecoin, Litecoin, and others. Litecoin is Bitcoin's closest competitor.

WHAT IS CRYPTOCURRENCY MINING?

As stated earlier, cryptocurrency uses a technique called cryptography to process transactions. This is a process that converts legible information into uncrackable codes that helps keep track of transfers and purchases. For a simple definition, it is just entries in a database that nobody can change without going through specific protocol.

Cryptography used the element of computer science and mathematical theory and was created during World War II to transfer information and data securely. It is now being used to secure money, information, and communications online.

Cryptocurrencies run on blockchains that are shared ledgers and get duplicated many times over a network of computers. An updated document gets made and distributed to anyone who holds cryptocurrency.

Each transaction that gets made and the owner of every cryptocurrency gets recorded onto the blockchain. These blockchains are run by miners that use very powerful computers to verify the transactions. They have to update every time a transaction gets made to ensure the information is authentic. This assures every transaction is processed safely, properly, and securely.

Miners get paid by minted cryptocurrency as payment for their work. These will show up as fees from merchants or vendors.

Cryptocurrency's value goes up and down based on supply and demand. It does not have a fixed value. Seller and buyers agree on a certain value that is fair based on what cryptocurrency is trading for elsewhere.

Transaction fees that are associated with credit cards are eliminated since the transaction is peer to peer. The identities of the seller and buyer are never revealed. Every transaction is public to everybody on the blockchain network.

People can get cryptocurrencies through exchanges online or trade it for normal currencies.

Mining for cryptocurrency has two functions: releasing new currency and adding transactions on the blockchain. Every block that gets added by miners has to contain proof of work.

Miners have to have a computer with a special program that helps them compete with other miners to solve complicated math problems. This takes large amounts of computer resources. Miners attempt to solve a block at regular intervals. They need the transaction's data and use hash functions to solve it.

The hash value is a value of numbers that can identify data. Miners use computers to find hash values less than the target. Whatever miner cracks it first is the one who actually mined the block and will get a reward. The reward for a block sits at 12.5 Bitcoins.

Early on, cryptography enthusiasts were the miners. As Bitcoin gained popularity and its value increased, mining is now a business on its own. Many businesses and people have begun investing in hardware and warehouses.

As businesses jumped on board, they soon realized they couldn't compete. Miners have started opening pools and combining their resources to compete better.

One business, Bank of New York Mellon Corp., has been using a blockchain platform since 2016 to help with US Treasury bond settlements. The privacy of the platform has allowed it to remain out of the grasp of regulatory agencies. When a bank decides to let its clients use it commercially, regulatory agencies might get into the action.

A mining kit contains a fan, cabling, memory, power supply, a processor, and graphics cards. The cost for this is around $2,400 to $3,800 if bought through Amazon. The best hardware for mining is AntMiner S9, AntMiner S7, and Avalon6.

Normal GPUs are not strong enough, so miners are beginning to use ASICs or application specific integrated circuits. To help with this shortcoming, AMD and Nvidia are working on GPUs that might be used just for this purpose.

There are two companies that are dominating the mining hardware, and they are Bitmain and Canaan. Bitmain is located in Beijing. It mines and manufactures hardware.

Mining Pools

Most mining pools are located in China and do about 81 percent of the hash rate. For Nvidia and AMD that dominate the gaming chip market, turning their focus off of their main business might not be a good course of action.

These companies have to create GPUs that were designed exclusively for the sole purpose of mining. These GPUs are a threat to the ASIC chips that are manufactured in China.

Exchanges and governments are contemplating about the regulations of cryptocurrencies. After MtGox, a Tokyo based exchange collapsed in 2014, Japan has introduced laws to protect users. Introducing taxes like a tax on capital gain of Bitcoin sales might slow down the cryptocurrency industry.

WHAT CAN YOU MINE?

Mining for cryptocurrencies and Bitcoin is very popular these days. As more people start mining, it gets harder to mine any type of cryptocurrency successfully.

To maximize your hashing power, you need to mine the currency that offers the most profit. Don't try to mine the difficult algorithms such as Bitcoin, try some easier cryptocurrencies. Once you have successfully mined the currency, convert it into the currency of your choice. You can do with by using an online exchange and thus maximizing profits.

Here are the cryptocurrencies that lead the pack:

- Bitcoin: With today's economy, each transaction we do has to go through the credit card company or a bank. They take out a fee for the transaction, and we have to hope they don't mess up. This is where Bitcoin comes in. At the center of Bitcoin are mathematical problems. Miners have to solve these. When a solution is found, the miner is rewarded with Bitcoins. Bitcoins are mined using powerful graphics cards.

- Ethereum: This platform is designed for people who want to create decentralized applications. In recent months, Ethereum has become very valuable and makes it the best choice for miners who are just beginning. It allows peer-to-peer transfer and a blockchain. This blockchain comes with its own language. This lets people use it for all sorts of decentralized applications. It is secured by cryptography. Ethereum doesn't have an ASIC. This doesn't mean you won't be able to make money. If you have a mining GPU, you can mine about $1,400 per year.

- Litecoin: This is another decentralized cryptocurrency. There is only about 84 million in existence. It offers low fees and quick transaction times. You can sell and buy it from other people and exchanges. You can use it to buy pretty much anything. If you use Antminer, you could mine about $6,000 per year.

- Dash: This is the first cryptocurrency that acts like fiat currency. You keep complete control of your money. You have total privacy, and there is no way to track the transactions. Transactions are processed instantly. There are virtually no fees since you control the money. Dash is one of three currencies that are most profitable. By mining using a specified ASIC, you could mine about $1,000 per year.

- Monero: This cryptocurrency is interchangeable. It prides itself on the privacy it gives to its users. Its value is increasing steadily. Investing in Monero hardware just might be the way to go. If you mine using a specified GPU, you could mine $1,400 per year.

- Zcash: This cryptocurrency is based on Bitcoin's platform but has one main difference. Zcash offers its users the option of encrypting their own transactions. This essentially means that the transaction's amount, the recipient's address, and the sender's address is all hidden from the public. Most think Zcash is the future of keeping transactions anonymous. Normal GPUs are able to mine Zcash like GTX 1080. It can also mine for Decred. Zcash has put a cap on how many coins can be mined. Jump in now as only 21 million will ever be mined.

- ZenCash: This cryptocurrency was made for user privacy. Most call it the privacy coin. All transactions are off the grid. This makes them extremely secure. It allows you to send coins straight to a recipient's address. This would be a great cryptocurrency to learn how to mine.

How It Works

Cryptocurrency creates blocks from all transactions. These get put together and creates a blockchain. Every time a transaction is done, the blockchain gets updated.

Miners use a process where they take the information and use formulas to process it. The result is a string of numbers and letters that is shorter than the actual transaction. This is known as a hash.

Every hash is similar to the hash that gets used first. Because every hash is based on the one in front of it, the next one will confirm the other ones were legitimate.

To mine for blocks, miners use specific GPUs to find answers to questions. When they find the answer, they receive a certain amount of coins as a reward. Miners use header metadata throughout the hash function. Each currency has its own algorithms. Litecoin uses Scrypt. Every time a valid hash gets found, it goes through the network and becomes part of the public ledger.

You are not able to fake your work and cheat. This is why all cryptocurrencies require proof of work. Ethereum is trying to get rid of proof of work and use proof of stake. If the miner can validate their work, they get rewarded with cryptocurrency.

Importance of an Efficient and Powerful GPU

Think about all the information that has been provided and you can understand why a powerful GPU is needed. You will be able to mine coins more successfully if you have a powerful GPU.

Powerful graphics cards use huge amounts of electricity. You need to think about how important the card's efficiency is as well. It might be better to buy several cheaper GPUs that have higher hash/power ratio. It might give you better profits. A good example of this type of GPU is the GTX 1050 Ti.

Mining is getting harder every day, so it is critical to have an efficient GPU. Some will cost you more in electricity bill than they will give you in revenue.

Factors That Harm the Efficiency of a Computer

You are not able to use just any graphics card to mine. Here are some cards to consider:

MHash/s

This is equivalent to how many numbers the card can handle during mining. You will use more hashes if you rate is high. If the hash rate is low, you won't use as many. What exactly does that mean? Higher hash rate means quicker results.

MHash/j

This is the number of hashes that the card can handle per energy joule. As stated earlier, mining uses a huge amount of electricity. Your graphics card will need to mine enough coins in order for you to make a profit after your electricity bill has been paid.

A larger number shows your card is more energy efficient. If the card is energy efficient, then you are saving yourself some money.

MHash/s/$

This is a way to show the performance/price ratio of a card. If it has a high number, you will get more for the money. If a card uses a lot of electricity and has a low hash rate, you won't be creating a lot of revenue, if any.

You need to find a card that has a good balance of performance and price. Mining for cryptocurrencies like Ethereum, Litecoin, and Bitcoin takes a very powerful graphics card. It actually takes several graphics cards. You will also need a motherboard that has the same amount of slots as GPU cards.

Make sure you have the correct power supply. If your computer doesn't have the right amount of power, it isn't going to work correctly.

Is Mining Right For You?

Mining is a great idea. Go out and purchase a mining GPI and watch the money roll in. Right?

Actually, no.

There are large warehouses in different countries that have very low electricity bills. These warehouses are home to thousands of GPUs, and the cost is anywhere from thousands to millions of dollars.

With this huge setup, mining is very profitable, and investors are making huge amounts of money. When an individual is mining on a personal computer at home, they might never see a return on their investment.

You can still benefit from mining. Some do it as a hobby that gives them a little something for their time. Unless you do it on a huge scale, you aren't going to see a whole lot of profits. If you just want to own some cryptocurrency, just purchase some.

Trading Cryptocurrency for USD or Other Cryptocurrencies

You will need to exchange your preferred cryptocurrency for Bitcoins first. Here is how to do it:

1. Create an account in an online exchange like Binance.

2. After the account has been created, now you will need to buy your preferred currency's wallet address. This address gets used with your mining software. The currency you mine gets put into this wallet. From there, you are able to exchange if for Bitcoin and then USD. To do this Hover over the tab that says Funds. A drop-down menu should appear. Now click on deposits/withdrawals. Look for your cryptocurrency and click on deposit. When asked, click agree and move on. You will be sent to a page that will show your personal address. Copy the code and put the software in this address.

3. After you have deposited cryptocurrency into your exchange account, you can decide to change it for Bitcoin. Here is how to do this:

   Go to the exchange's homepage but clicking on the logo. Go to the BTC Markets and look for your cryptocurrency. When you have chosen your currency, you will see it in the search results. Click on it. In the sell box, you can exchange your currency for Bitcoin. If you need to convert all the currency you own into Bitcoin, just choose 100 percent.

4. Now, you will need to transfer your Bitcoins out of the exchange you are using into another one like Gemini or Coinbase. After it has been transferred, you can exchange Bitcoins for USD. Here is how to do it:

   Go back to the deposits/withdrawals page. You can now withdraw your acquired Bitcoins out of your Bitcoin wallet like this:

   Type in your Bitcoin address. Go to either Gemini or Coinbase (whichever one you used). When you have finished the registration, now click on accounts. Click receive under the BTC wallet. You should see a QR code pop up. This is your wallet's address. You will need to copy and paste this into the BTC withdrawal address. Choose your amount and then submit.

5. The final step is to sell you Bitcoin for normal currency. Go to the sell/buy tab and click on sell. Just choose the bank or account you want the money deposited into. Type in the amount of Bitcoin you want to deposit and click sell Bitcoin. That's it.

You have successfully traded your cryptocurrency for Bitcoin and exchanged Bitcoin for USD.

For this chapter, we are going to get into the nitty-gritty of building your rig and mining. For the purpose of this chapter, we will look at building and Ethereum rig. This will go through sourcing your equipment as well as putting it together. This could take you up to a week to accomplish. You also have the option of buying a cloud mining contract through Genesis Mining or Hashflare if you are not interested in buying mining equipment.

Sourcing Equipment

You need to get a hold of a lot of components, and the costs can stack up.

1. Motherboard

The brain of your computer, the motherboard is what everything is built into and the base of your rig. The main thing you need to look at for your motherboard is how many GPU slots it has because this will determine how many GPU's or graphics cards it can hold, which is what determines your hashing power. If the motherboard has 3 PCI Express slots, then you will be able to fit 3 x Radeon HD 7950 and have a hash rate of 20 MH/s each, which will give you a complete hashing power of 60 MH/s. The PCI Express slot is the connection spot on your motherboard. They are typically white, but they may be beige. There are other types of slots but for the most part GPU's work on PCI.

2. Graphics card

Now you pick your GPUs. There are some graphics cards out there that will cost you an arm and a leg, but they have horrible hashing power. Then there are others that are more reasonably priced and have more power. You basically need to find a balance between the power you are looking for and how much you are willing to spend. The important thing is that you pick an efficient GPU. You can purchase refurbished GPUs from reputable sites like GPU shack. You have to be careful though; there are a lot of second-hand cards that have problems that you won't discover until you plug them in.

There is one common issue that you can have with your motherboard and graphics card. You may find that they don't all fit together perfectly because of how the PCI Express slots are spaced on the motherboard. Fear not, you can get a riser which works like an extension cable for the slot. There are some graphics cards that are bulky, so be careful when you are choosing your card.

3. Hard drive

The hard drive is needed for you to store your operating system and the mining software on. You can use a standard SSD drive. The size you need will depend on what you want to do when you are mining. If you are interested in downloading the complete blockchain, then you need to consider how large the blockchain will become and the time you need to spend on it. If you plan on mining Ethereum as part of a pool than you won't have to store the blockchain and you will be able to get a smaller SSD drive.

4. RAM

This is one of the most basic components of all computers and works as a scratchpad for writing down calculations and being able to call that information up quickly on your computer. 4GB should be big enough.

5. PSU

You can get power supply units in several different sizes, and this can cause problems for some when they are trying to figure out the size they need. You should add up your GPU's power consumption and all of your other components, and then make sure that that the power supply has a bigger power supply. If you are using two GPUs that use 220 watts and your other components take up another 250 watts, then you can use a 750-watt power supply unit because the complete amount of power you need is only 690 watts. If you plan on building a "mega rig" that contains six GPU's, you may find that it is more cost efficient to use two different power supplies. Two 750 watt PSU at the cost of $100 a piece is better than $300 for a single 1500 watt PSU.

6. A case

This can prove to be fairly difficult choice because it will depend on your GPU's, as well as whether or not you are using risers. You need to make sure you don't have components sitting on top of one another as this is a fire hazard. You can choose to leave your system open air; you can build a case for it yourself to give it a little personalization. You can also choose to buy an off the shelf rig from a few providers. They can take awhile to get to you, but all of the hard work is done.

gpuShack.com is a great website to source your components. They offer group packages, which can make it cheaper for you.

Putting Your Rig Together

Like I said earlier, you need to make sure that your power supply will be able to handle your graphics cards, and then you also have risers that will give you the chance to place extra GPU's in safe place. All of the connections need to be plugged in correctly and that everything is held together.

A word of advice on positioning, GPU's can become hot, especially if they are overclocked, so you need to make sure you get the best bang for your buck. You also need to make sure that your rig is placed in a well-ventilated area so that you don't risk it overheating.

Once your rig is turned on, you will want to make sure that all of the software you need for mining is on your rig.

Software

The first thing you have to do is to install an operating system onto your rig. For people who are more technically minded, you can use Linux Ubuntu, but for most people, Windows is the best choice because it automates installing drivers so that all of the components talk correctly to each other. The best part of Ubuntu, though, is it provides a lot of options and its free.

You can also choose to download EthOs, which is an APP that was specifically designed for Ethereum mining. This is the perfect way a specific mining system for your GPU's and rigs to manage all of them.

After you have downloaded your operating system onto your rig, there are two ways that you are able to start mining:

• Solo mining – this type of mining means that it is you against everybody else. If you create the correct hash, then you will get the block reward. If you have a rig of 60 MH/s and a hashing power of 1.2 GH, you probably won't see much ether. You will also need to download the blockchain.

• Pool mining – this type of mining requires you to team up with other miners to lower the volatility of returns. This could mean that you get five ether every five days, or you get an ether every single day. The best thing about this is that you get a continued stream of ether and you won't need to download the complete blockchain.

Mining Ethereum

You should now have a pretty good understanding of how mining works, so you are probably itching to get started mining yourself. As a little refresher, mining is what holds the 'decentralized app store' together by making sure that there is a consensus for every change to the applications that are running on the network.

Take, for example, the online notebook that is described in "What is Ethereum?" The network was unable to reach a consensus about the notebook's state, as if a note was deleted or added, without computational power to process through the changes.

Miners allow their computers to go crazy to solve cryptographic puzzles in an attempt to get ether, and they need to try a large number of computational problems until somebody can unlock a new asset batch.

A very interesting part of an open blockchain is that, theoretically, anybody can set their computers to only focus on these puzzles as a way for them to win the mining rewards. The problem is that mining on these public blockchains will eventually require even more power over a period of time as more people begin investing in better hardware.

It is now very unlikely for those that are mining with low-powered setups for them to win, but it is still a pretty decent past-time for enthusiast and hobbyists.

As you learned earlier, you need a rig that is solely used for mining. You can choose from GPUs and CPUs, as you know. GPUs will provide you with a better has rated. GPUs are the only option for a person that is interested in mining ether.

Getting your GPU together can be quite complex, so make sure that you get others advice, and don't rely only on this book. Other people may have good advice on the most profitable choices based on hash rate, initial expense, and power consumption.

You can also find mining profitability calculators that will show how much you may be able to earn given your hash rate when set against the electricity cost and setup.

After you have set up your rig, and have taken care of your hardware, you need to get your software ready. Miners will need to install a client that can connect to the network. People who are familiar with a command line can choose to install geth, which will run an ethereum node written in 'Go,' a scripting language.

After you have your software downloaded, your node will be able to talk with other nodes, which will connect it to the Ethereum network. Besides the fact that it can be used to mine ether, it will give you the interface to deploy smart contracts and send transactions with a command line.

Testing

You can also choose to mine 'test' ether on a private network so that you can experiment with the decentralized applications or smart contracts. Mining on a test network won't require fancy hardware on your part. All you will need is a home computer with geth or some other client installed. Minting fake ether isn't going to be all that lucrative.

Install Ethminer

If you are planning on mining real ether, you need to install mining software. After you have downloaded a client and your node has become a part of the network, you will then need to download Ethminer. You will need to find the right download version for your operating system.

After this has been installed, your node will start to play a part in staking your place in the Ethereum network.

Join a Mining Pool

You probably won't be that successful as a sole miner of ether. This is why there are miner pools. Miners 'pool' their computational power together to create a mining pool. This will improve the chances of solving the puzzles and getting a reward for everybody involved in the pool. They will then split their profits proportional to the amount of power the miner contributed.

There are a lot of different factors that are involved in jumping into a mining pool. Every pool probably won't stay around for forever, and the computational power of all of these pools change constantly, so there are a few factors that you need to consider before you decide to join one.

One important thing that you need to remember is that mining pools have different types of payout structures. A mining pool will a signup process on their website so that miners are able to connect with the pool and then start mining.

You have to remember the world of mining is a whirlwind of change. The tools that you learn today could disappear next year, and there are mining pools that may fall away while others are created, so you have to keep an eye out for industry shifts.

Mining Bitcoin

Mining Bitcoin works pretty much the same as mining Ethereum. You will need to have you mining rig set up and ready to go. For the most part, you will probably need to make sure you get an ASIC if you are interested in mining Bitcoin. Otherwise, you probably aren't going to see much in return. You will then need to download the mining software. There are a lot of programs that you can use for Bitcoin, but the most popular choices are BFGminer and CGminer which work as command line programs.

If you want the ease of use that you can get with a GUI, then you may want to download EasyMiner, which works as a click and go Android/Windows/Linux program.

After you have everything ready to start mining, it is best that you join a Bitcoin mining pool. Without using a mining pool, you might be stuck mining Bitcoins for years and never earn a single one. It's a lot easier to share the work and then split the reward a group of miners.

If you want a fully decentralized pool, you can use p2pool. As of right now, the following pools fully validate block using the Bitcoin core 0.9.5 or later:

• Slush Pool
• Eligius
• CK Pool
• BitMinter

No matter what coin you are mining, you will need to make sure that you have a wallet for your coins to be deposited in. Above all else, make sure that you stay up to date on all the current Bitcoin news. This is important for your profits.

Writing Script

If you are planning on using cpuminer, you will need to know how to set up your parameters for mining. It's easier to create a one-line script, called a batch file in Windows, to launch your miner with the right instructions.

For this you will need:

• Worker password

- Worker number or name
- Mining pool username
- Port number for the server
- Stratum URL for the mining pool server
- Full path to the directory where your program is stored

You will then need to open Notepad or your text editor of choice. You should not ever use a word processor like MS word. Next, you will need to type in the script. This method assumes that you are trying to mine a currency that uses the scrypt algorithm.

Start "path" minerd.exe – url URL:PORT –a scrypt - - userpass USERNAME.WORKER:PASSWORD

When you type in the above details, you should get the following:

Start "C:|cpu-miner-pooler" minerd.exe –url stratum+tcp:// pool.d2.cc:3333 –a scrypt – userpass username.1:x

You will then need to save this file with a ".bat" extension. After you have saved the batch file, double-click it to activate your new miner program. The mining pool is probably going to have a web-based interface. After a few minutes, the website should start to show that you are actively mining.

GPU Miner Setup

For those that you interested in mining with GPUs, which would be anybody that creates a mining rig, you should use the cgminer program. Versions of cgminer past 3.72, do not support scrypt mining, this means that you shouldn't just download the latest version. You will need to find the version that offers everything you need.

This setup is assuming you are using Windows. If you are using OS X or Linus, the command line arguments are going to be the same.

You need to extract the software into a folder that you are able to find easily. You now need to make sure that your graphics drivers are up to date. You then need to press the Windows key with the "R" key. Then type in the "cmd," and then select enter. This will give you a command terminal. You can then use the "cd" command to switch the directory to the one that has the cgminer file.

Type in "cgminer.exe –n." This will give you the list of the recognized devices on your PC. If it can detect your graphics card, then you can go to the next step. If it does not detect your graphics card, then you need to research the steps required for properly setting up your graphics card. Then make sure you have the information for your mining pool. This is the same information that you needed for the CPU setup.

Now you need to create a batch file so that you can start your cgminer correctly.

Start "path" cgminer – scrypt –o URL:PORT –u USERNAME. WORKER –p PASSWORD

Now you have your chosen mining software set up, you will start to see statistics scrolling through the command line. If you have cgminer, you are going to get more info than that with cpuminer. With the cgminer, you will see information about the mining hardware, mining pool, and currency. If you are using cpuminer, you are only going to see information about the blocks that your computer has solved, and your hashing speed.

The great thing for people who have a PC with dedicated graphics cards, you can run cgminer and cpuminer together. To this, you will add a "-threads n" argument into the minerd command. In this, the "n" stands for the number of CPU cores that you want to employ.

You need to make sure that you leave a few of these cores free to work your GPUs. If you set minerd to use all of your CPU cores your CPU will be too busy to send data to the GPU. If you have a quad core CPU, then you should set the argument to "2" or "3."

When you mine with CPU and GPU, you will be able to see how much better GPUs are when it comes to mining. Look at the hash rates in your terminal window for your programs, and you will likely see at least five times the difference.

DUMP FOR DOLLARS, OR KEEP THE CRYPTOCURRENCY

One of the biggest questions people will ask is which cryptocurrency they should buy. Another commonality for the beginner is that they don't spend most of their day listing to the options of cryptocurrency experts and personalities, doing extensive research, and analyzing the market.

Even if there is some seemingly knowledgeable and trustworthy "expert" that tells you that you need to invest in cryptocurrency A or B, a beginner doesn't have the business experience or technical skills to evaluate if this is or isn't a person that you can trust.

One thing is for certain; beginners aren't interested in getting into a coin that has huge volatility and an unknown future. This means that it only makes sense for them to get into coins that are built on solid tech, a strong team, and solid business plan.

When you have mined or bought cryptocurrencies, there are few things to look at so that you can figure out if you should keep it or sell it for dollars:

- Is there a highly reputable team backing this coin?
- How active are they in improving and maintaining their coin?
- Are they actively communicating with their investors?
- Is the coin blockchain based?
- How many coins are in circulation and what is a total number of coins?
- How much are they worth?
- How many coins were premined and are you able to mine them?

- How many exchanges have these coins?

Now that we have gone through some important steps you should take, let's look at the coins that I would suggest holding onto. This should not be used as investment advice; it's only an opinion.

Steem

This cryptocurrency is used on the social media blogging platform Steemit. They also have a Steem dollar, which means they have two cryptocurrencies. The Steem dollar will only ever be worth a dollar, whereas Steem's value will depend on the market.

I believe most of its value comes from Steemit. Platforms such as Twitter and Facebook aren't incentivized. You have a greater chance having to pay them to use the site, than making money from it. Steemit gives you the chance to make Steem dollars and Steem by posting quality content. You can blog for money on Steemit, but the upvotes you receive for your content is what determines the amount you earn.

You can also power up your Steem by using Steem power. Steem power is what decided the worth of your vote. If you were to have 1,000 Steem power, your upvote would be worth 20 cents. But, if you have 500,000 Steem power, the upvote would worth $100. Basically, you are encouraged to spend money on Steemit.

If you want to withdraw money, you will have to wait three months to power down. This keeps people from being able to move money away from Steemit, which keeps the value of Steemit.

Ark

Ark is known for their SmartBridge technology. This technology allows people to link different blockchains together through their bridging method. Think about linking together the Lisk blockchain and Ethereum blockchain.

Their team is also pretty competent. Some of them have helped develop Crypti and Lisk. They also have other amazing features like an interplanetary file system, physical card system, optional privacy, and fast transaction speed. It's a coin that looks to be on the rise.

Siacoin

Currently ranked in the top 40 of cryptocurrencies, Siacoin has a market cap of just higher than $200 million. 28 billion Siacoins are in circulation, and it will quickly reach its cap of over 40 billion.

The value of this coin comes from the fact that it is one of the few coins that have a product. It has a decentralized storage space that has better safeguards from hackers when compared to the other mainstream cloud services. It will likely be able to compete with cloud storages provided by Google Drive, Microsoft Dropbox, and Amazon S3, at a lower price. The price for their service will be affected by the market forces.

Paying less for cloud storage is what Siacoin hopes to achieve. You need 2,000 Siacoins to be able to use this service. You will also get the chance to rent out space to others. Since the coins and storage are limited, the value will definitely increase.

It does have some competition with Storj and Maid Safe coin.

Monero

Monero has better anonymity than Bitcoin, which is the reason why its worth was able to go up from $50 to $125 in only a few days. The biggest reason to keep Monero is the user anonymity. There are a lot of sophisticated and intricate methods to create this privacy. It can be broken down into several different methods.

It makes use of a stealth address. If you trade with other types of coins, you will probably see a destination address, and this means that others are able to track you. Monero only displays cryptographic hashes for the destination address. The recipient and sender are the only two people who can read the hash.

They make use of separate transaction units. Let's say you send 100 XMR; it will be delivered to the recipient in separate sums of 30, 20, and 50 XMR. They are each recoded separately, making it harder to track. They also use ring signatures to mix up the transactions and to make anonymity possible.

Ethereum

Ethereum is seen as the best alternative to Bitcoin, and you can see this in its price. In September 2017 it traded at $380. The biggest success for Ethereum is its introduction of the Ethereum network. It made programming on blockchain a lot easier, and this is the reason why there are so many popular coins that are based on this network. Golem and OmiseGo are two great options.

Smart contracts are another reason why Ethereum is so popular. Bitcoin's smart contract consists of sending and receiving coins. Ethereum's smart contracts take things to a whole new level. It gives people the change to manage agreements and makes sure that a payment is made when it is supposed to be.

OmiseGo

This coin is based in Thailand and provides Southeast Asia Stripe-like payment features. The coin is based on Ethereum's network, and it provides the user with real-time payment services and value exchange across jurisdictions. It also lets a user exchange both cryptocurrencies and fiat currencies.

Holders of OMG will be able to make money through transaction fees. The more transactions there are, the more money a holder will make. Because of this, the price of OMG will rise.

The best part of OMG is their financial transaction, which includes business to business commerce, payments, loyalty programs, remittances, and more. They are also done in an inexpensive way.

Iota

As of right now, Iota is the only coin that isn't based on blockchain. It has a new data transfer and transactional settlement layer for the internet of things. The coin is based on a distributed ledger known as Tangle, and its goal is to overcome the problems of blockchain.

Theoretically, it has no transaction fees, unlimited transaction rate, and no miners. This means that it does not have a scalability problem. It also gives people the chance to use small nanopayments. You are also unable to split a coin.

So What Should You Do?

With digital currencies, nobody can be for certain. There is always a risk when getting involved in cryptocurrencies, especially if you choose to invest in them. There is a chance that a $50 coin could end up being worth 50 cents the next day. The listed coins above have a good chance of continuing to rise in value, which means it is a good idea to hold them. As far as selling them for a fiat currency, that comes down to you. Keep an eye on the market to see how things are looking for the coin, and then decide whether you would be better off keeping it or selling it.

FUTURE OF
CRYPTOCURRENCY

Cryptocurrencies were able to make the jump from an academic concept to reality when Bitcoin was launched in 2009. Bitcoin continued to attract more followers in the subsequent years, and in 2013 in caught the attention of the media and investors when it hit a record of $266 per Bitcoin. Bitcoin has carried a market value of more than two billion dollars at its peak, but then it experienced a 50% plunge, which caused a raging debate about the cryptocurrencies future. Are these currencies going to supplant conventional currencies and become as universal as the euro and dollar? Or are they more of a passing fad that will fade away in a few years? Bitcoin seems to hold the answer.

The Current Standard

The decentralized nature of Bitcoin makes it free from interference or manipulation of the government. It also means that there isn't a central authority to make sure that everything runs smoothly or anything to back its value. The digital coins are created through mining that requires computers to figure out complex algorithms. The current rate of creation is 25 Bitcoins every ten minutes, and the amount is capped at 21 million, which is expected to be reached in the year 2140.

This is what makes Bitcoin so different from the regular fiat currencies, which has the backing of its government. Fiat currencies are centralized and supervised by a central bank of a nation. While a bank is in control of how much of the currency is given in accordance with the policy, there isn't an upper limit to how much can be issued. Deposits are typically insured against any failures of the bank by a governing body. Bitcoin does not have any of these support mechanisms. Bitcoin's value is completely dependent on what investors will pay for it at any given time. If a Bitcoin exchange were to fold up, the people who have Bitcoin balances have no way of getting them back.

The transaction anonymity and decentralization benefits of Bitcoin have also made it a favorite payment for a lot of illegal activity, which include weapons procurement, smuggling, drug peddling, and money laundering. This has caused it to attract the attention of government agencies like the SEC, Financial Crimes Enforcement Network, Department of Homeland Security, and FBI. The FinCEN issued new rules in March 2013 that defined these virtual administrators and exchanges as money service businesses, which brought them within the scope of government regulation. In May of the same year, the DHS froze a Mt. Gox account that was held at Wells Fargo, saying that anti-money laundering laws were broke. Then on August, 22 emerging payment companies were issued subpoenas by New York's Department of Financial Services. Many of these companies handled Bitcoin. The subpoenas looked to find out the measures they were taking to prevent money laundering, and how they would ensure consumer protection.

Bitcoin Alternatives

Despite the issues it has had, Bitcoin's growing visibility and success has caused several companies to unveil alternative coins, like:

- Litecoin – presently, this altcoin is seen as Bitcoin's biggest rival. It was created to process small transactions faster. Unlike the computer horsepower you need for Bitcoin, Litecoin can be mined using a normal computer. Litecoin has a max of 84 million coins, which is four times more than Bitcoin's limit.

- Ripple – OpenCoin launched Ripple. The payment

mechanism for Ripple allows for funds transfers in any currency to a Ripple use in a matter of seconds, which is a big difference to Bitcoin's ten-minute confirmation.

- MintChip – Unlike most other altcoins, MintChip was created by a government institution. This currency is a smart card that has an electronic value, and it can be transferred between chips. MintChip does not require any personal identification, but it is backed by the Canadian dollar.

The Future

The current limitations that cryptocurrencies face, like a person's digital fortune being erased by a crash, or a virtual vault being ransacked by a hacker, could be overcome in time with new advances. What's harder to fix is the paradox of cryptocurrencies: the more they grow in popularity, the more government regulation and scrutiny that will attract, which will eventually erode the fundamental purpose.

While there may be a growing number of merchants who accept these cryptocurrencies, they are still a minority. For them to become used more widely, they will need to gain widespread acceptance among their users. Their complexity, when compared to other currencies, will probably deter people, except for those that are technically adept.

A cryptocurrency that is looking to become part of the mainstream financial world will have to satisfy a wide array of criteria. It will need to be mathematically complex to fight off hackers, but easy enough for the regular consumer to understand. It should be decentralized, but have enough safeguards for consumer protection. It also needs to keep user anonymity without it being used for money laundering, tax evasion, and other illegal activities.

Since all of this is a lot to satisfy, there is a chance that some of the popular cryptocurrencies out there, in a few years, could develop attributes that lie between today's cryptocurrencies and regulated fiat currencies. While this seems like a remote possibility, there is very little doubt that Bitcoin's success in handling these challenges may determine the outlook for altcoins in the coming years.

CONCLUSION

Thanks for making it through to the end of *Cryptocurrency Mining*. Let's hope it was informative and able to provide you with all of the tools you need to achieve your goals.

The next step is to use the information you have learned to help you start your mining rig. Mining cryptocurrencies can be very rewarding if you do things the right way. Continue to research more, and become an amazing miner.

Finally, if you found this book useful in any way, a review on Amazon is always appreciated!